NOTRE~DAME DE PARIS

(BEFORE THE FIRE)

ROOSTER ATOP THE

ROSE WINDOW

SPIRE

ROSE WINDOW

BEES!

SACRISTY

ONE OF THE SIXTEEN STATUES SURROUNDING THE SPIRE

SPIRE

TO LINDA URBAN AND JANE KURTZ
FOR LENDING ME THEIR COURAGE, AND ESPECIALLY
TO GREG FOR THE WINGS TO FLY —M.P.B.

TO EVERY LITTLE BEE, AND MARGARET —E.B.G.

Text copyright © 2023 by Meghan P. Browne

Jacket and cover art copyright © 2023 by E. B. Goodale

All rights reserved. Published in the United States by Random House Studio, an imprint of Random House

Children's Books, a division of Penguin Random House LLC, New York.

Random House Studio with colophon is a registered trademark of Penguin Random House LLC.

Visit us on the Web! rhcbooks.com

Educators and librarians, for a variety of teaching tools, visit us at RHTeachersLibrarians.com

Library of Congress Cataloging-in-Publication Data is available upon request.

ISBN 978-0-593-37456-6 (trade) — ISBN 978-0-593-37457-3 (lib. bdg.) — ISBN 978-0-593-37458-0 (ebook)

The text of this book is set in 13.2-point TT Ramillas Medium.

The illustrations were rendered in monoprint, oil paint, gouache, collage, and colored pencils.

Book design by Rachael Cole

MANUFACTURED IN CHINA

10 9 8 7 6 5 4 3 2 1

First Edition

⸎ THE **BEES** OF ⸎
NOTRE-DAME

BY **MEGHAN P. BROWNE**
ILLUSTRATED BY **E. B. GOODALE**

RANDOM HOUSE STUDIO ⌂ NEW YORK

When spring arrives in Paris, people pop up like
tulips from underground after working, riding, and
resting through short winter days.

Dawn breaks earlier each morning. The sun says,
"Come!
Walk in the streets to feel my warmth on your face.
Smell the buttery croissants.
Hear the accordion's song."

High above cobblestone streets
Sibyle's bellows bloom.

FOOSH · FOOSH

"Bonjour, les filles!"
All winter long the bees rested, waited,
and warmed each other until . . .

. . . one April morning, the sun pushes
the chill from the air and says,
"Come!
Stretch your wings wide.
Gather pollen in your pockets
and nectar in your belly!
Make the colony strong with new life!"

Cotton-soft tree seeds float like snow.

A hopeful breeze drives children's boats.

A pigeon tucks into a topiary tree to build
her nest out of sight.

Higher than the rooftops and the treetops,
up past the tip-top of the tower . . .

. . . a young queen takes her mating flight
and returns home.

Beneath the roof of a small pine box, workers
dance to show a map of the sweetest gardens
in Paris, and the queen lays her eggs—
one by one—in thousands of perfect hexagons
waxed by generations of bees
that came before her.

Far below,
people celebrate,
admire, and stand in a holy hush.
Around and above them:
stones that had to be dug
and carved—
trees that had to be axed
and raised—
glass that had to be stained
and lifted.
Thousands of hands
worked together
for hundreds of years
to make something amazing
under the great spire.

On the rooftop, worker bees bring pollen and nectar from gardens
across the city and fill row after row with every shade of sunshine.

Nurse bees tend to tiny eggs . . .
that turn into curly larvae . . .
and grow into colorless pupae
under a papery cap.

Then everything changes.

CRICK-CRACK-CRACKLE
Sparks fall.

EEEEOOOO·EEEEOOOO
Sirens scream.

And when the spire falls,
the whole world cries.

WHOOSH-WHOOSH!

Fireboats pump chilly river water up, up, up
through snaking hoses.

PSSSSHH-PSSSSHH!

Water cannons blast.
Firefighters battle heat and smoke
to quench the flames, to save the cathedral.
To save the hives.

The cathedral smolders under ashes and ruin.

This cathedral has outlived kings and queens and
emperors, survived neglect and looting, and witnessed
wars and disease and destruction too dark to be forgotten.

When the tall black cloud of smoke and ash finally clears,
the sun rises to say,
"Come!
Rebuild.
Work with each other.
You are stronger together.

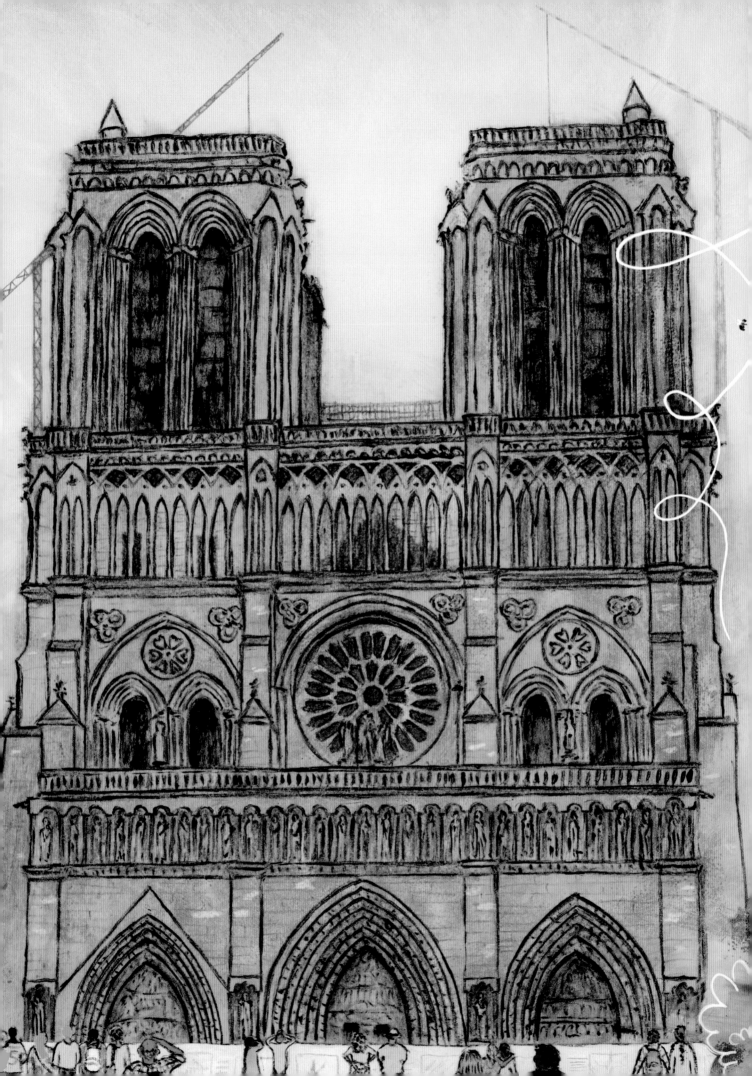

"Just like the bees."

MORE ABOUT THE STORY

On April 15, 2019, with the last Mass of Holy Monday underway, an electrical fire started silently in the ancient roof of the great Notre-Dame Cathedral in Paris. Flames and smoke soon grew beyond control. Shocked Parisians filled the streets, and people around the world stared in horror at video streams. Sibyle Moulin watched the cathedral burn and hoped that the bees she cared for atop the sacristy at Notre-Dame were safe.

Sibyle Moulin

Author and beekeeper Meghan P. Browne shadows Sibyle Moulin during her workday on April 26, 2019, just days after the catastrophic fire at Notre-Dame.

Margaret Chiarelli

Illustrator E. B. Goodale sketching while sitting on the bank of the Seine River, looking at the south side of Notre-Dame in 2022.

For days, the world watched and waited to hear what could be salvaged from the destruction. Sibyle wasn't the only one worried about the bees. By week's end, reporters from international news outlets were begging to know the fate of the bees of Notre-Dame. On Good Friday, a drone flew above the charred church and captured images showing the hive boxes upright and untouched by the flames. Disaster and despair turned to relief and hope. Thanks in great part to the skill and preparedness of the Paris Fire Brigade, the bees had survived. Despite the tragic fire, the bees, the cathedral, and Paris would go on.

Beekeepers like Sibyle tend to rooftop honeybee hives above the bustling streets of Paris. They care for bees that live on roofs and terraces in the financial district and at offices of international companies, cultural community centers, and government agencies, as well as at private residences.

Their job is hard work: Sibyle maneuvers heavy beehives through crowded streets and climbs ladders carrying boxes full of insects. She wears a beekeeping suit with a veil, but Sibyle most often conducts her hive inspections with ungloved hands in order to work with the most care and precision. She does her job in rain or shine, even though bad weather can make the bees grumpy. Sibyle takes meticulous notes and makes important decisions to keep the colonies healthy, peaceful, and strong.

The reconstruction and restoration of the Notre-Dame Cathedral has been the work of many, many hands. Every decision is diligently debated, calculated, and executed by skilled engineers, foresters, carpenters, organists, historians, and other experts. The French government hopes to reopen the cathedral in time for the Paris 2024 Summer Olympic Games, but the work will not stop then. Just as thousands of tradespeople built the ancient cathedral over generations, it will take thousands more workers and many more years to rebuild and repair what the fire destroyed.

Beekeeper Sibyle Moulin conducts hive inspections on the rooftop of the Notre-Dame sacristy in 2018.

Though the bees no longer sit atop the cathedral, Sibyle still cares for the pollinators in a street-level garden outside the sacristy. Bees and other pollinators play an important role in maintaining biodiversity around the world. Since 2012, the city of Paris has supported beekeepers tending to hives across the city: in hidden park gardens, tucked away in courtyards and on balconies, and high above it all on the rooftops. The bees and the keepers work out of sight and beyond the attention of most people, but their efforts make Paris one of the world's most vibrant cities.

SPECIAL THANKS

The author and illustrator are indebted to beekeepers Sibyle Moulin and Nicolas Géant of Alvéole, whose kindness, generosity, and expertise made this book possible. Thank you also to entomologist Ashley Mortensen, PhD, for her expertise and keen eye for detail.

RECOMMENDED READING

Burns, Loree Griffin, with photographs by Ellen Harasimowicz. *Honeybee Rescue: A Backyard Drama.* Watertown, MA: Charlesbridge, 2022.

Fleming, Candace, and Eric Rohmann. *Honeybee: The Busy Life of Apis Mellifera.* New York: Neal Porter Books, 2020.

"France's Seine River Is a Place of Solace during COVID-19 Pandemic." *Morning Edition,* NPR, 4 Jan. 2021. npr.org/2021/01/04/953146912/frances-seine-river-is-a-place-of-solace-during -covid-19-pandemic

Hugo, Victor. *The Hunchback of Notre-Dame.* Translated by Isabel Florence Hapgood (1850–1928). Berkeley, CA: Mint Editions, 2020.

"Rebuild, Restore Notre-Dame." Friends of Notre-Dame de Paris, 21 Oct. 2022. friendsofnotredamedeparis.org

Sciolino, Elaine. *The Seine: The River That Made Paris.* New York: W. W. Norton, 2019.

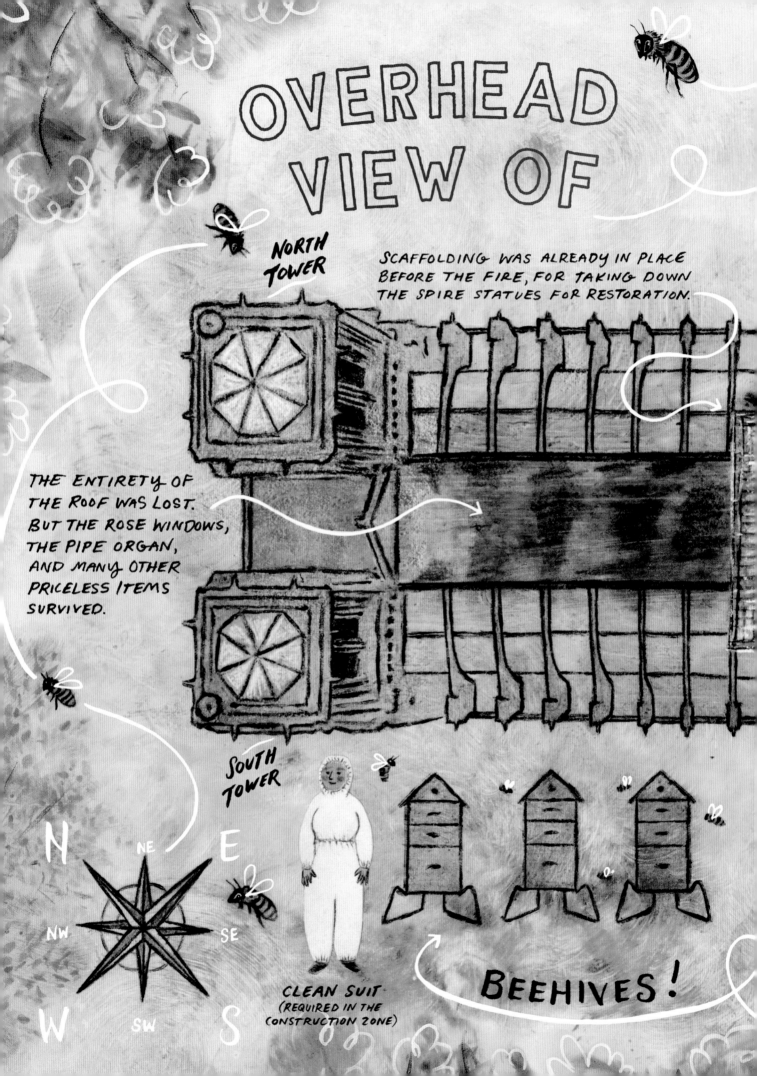

OVERHEAD VIEW OF

NORTH TOWER

SCAFFOLDING WAS ALREADY IN PLACE BEFORE THE FIRE, FOR TAKING DOWN THE SPIRE STATUES FOR RESTORATION.

THE ENTIRETY OF THE ROOF WAS LOST. BUT THE ROSE WINDOWS, THE PIPE ORGAN, AND MANY OTHER PRICELESS ITEMS SURVIVED.

SOUTH TOWER

CLEAN SUIT (REQUIRED IN THE CONSTRUCTION ZONE)

BEEHIVES!

N NE E NW SE W SE S SW